A Nineveh Moment

Does America Have Another Chance?

Dr. David Schnittger, D. Min., President

Southwest Prophecy Ministries

www.swpm.us

A Nineveh Moment

By David Schnittger, D. Min.

Printed in the United States of America

ISBN: 978-1-0812-2881-1

Unless otherwise indicated, Bible quotations are taken from the King James Version

Table of Contents

Foreword

"This will not end peacefully." This was my conclusion when Ron Paul was denied the Republican Presidential nomination in 2012 by the Republican establishment. As an ardent member of the "Ron Paul Revolution" in both 2008 and 2012, I was convinced that Dr. Paul was America's last best hope for restoring America as a Christian Constitutional Republic. With his defeat and retirement from public office, I despaired that nothing short of a bloody revolution by America's patriots would ever restore the Republic.

Fast forward four years to September 2015. The Republican primaries had just begun. A newcomer to politics, Donald Trump, was scheduled to speak at the Oklahoma State Fairgrounds. More out of curiosity than anything, I decided to go. I was not the only one. When I arrived at the open-air bandstand two hours in advance of the scheduled appearance, the place was packed with thousands of Okies, standing patiently in anticipation of "the Donald." When he appeared, the place went CRAZY! He had the audience in the palm of his hand as he spoke simply but forcefully of the need to secure our borders and bring back American jobs.

I have listened to politicians my whole adult life, but this man was different. He was one of us, saying out loud what so many hard-working Americans are afraid to say: "The ruling class does not care about us!" After much observation and contemplation, I have come to the conclusion that God is extending to America a "Nineveh Moment," a gracious time for repentance and restoration. This book is about the amazing "movement" that Donald Trump is giving voice to, a Second American Revolution . . . a movement that is bringing "A Nineveh Moment" to America!

The "Nineveh Moment" was interrupted by the stolen election of 2020. After three years of the disastrous Biden regime, we are now facing the final battle for our Republic. How we respond will determine the fate of "History's Great Nation."

Dr. David Schnittger

Chapter One

IS AMERICA IN BIBLE PROPHECY?

It is important, at the outset of our consideration as to whether America is in the midst of a "Nineveh Moment," to ponder the question as to whether America has a place in Bible prophecy. If America is merely an "exceptional" country, as some politicians and preachers declare today, then there is no reason to believe that God would go out of His way to extend mercy to America in an unusual way. However, if the Bible predicts that America will have a unique role in the last days, then there is a biblical basis for arguing for "a Nineveh moment" for America.

In fact, there are some contemporary Christian authors who confidently deny that America is the subject of Bible prophecy. For example, celebrated prophecy expert Mark Hitchcock published two books denying America is in the Bible. The first, *Is America in Bible Prophecy?* was published nine months after 9/11 (2002) and *The Late Great United States: What Bible Prophecy Reveals About America's Last Days* (2009) are both a great disappointment to those expecting to find where America is in Bible prophecy.

This modern denial of America's unique role in Bible prophecy was foreign to many of America's earliest explorers and founders. Consider, for example, historian Ruth Bloch's view as expressed in her book, *Visionary Republic*: "End times prophecy beliefs were basic to the formation of American Revolutionary idolatry." Famed historian Arthur Schlesinger Jr. stated in a bicentennial speech to the 1976 American Historical Association: "The new land was certainly a part, perhaps the climax, of redemptive history; America was divine prophecy fulfilled."

The Idea of America Being Predicted in the Bible Began With the Colonization of America

The idea that America is forecast in the Bible has a genealogy going back to the discoverer of the New World, Christopher Columbus. He was the first to say that the gigantic landmass he uncovered that was hidden from the civilized world for millennia was predicted in Bible prophecy. His view was that his discovery was not merely the fulfillment of Bible prophecy, but the beginning of the Last Days before Christ's Second Coming.

The idea that Columbus spearheaded, namely, God's prophecy of America, electrified American colonial leaders up to, during and after the American Revolution. Columbus was regarded as the first prophet of America and "Columbia" became a nickname for the new nation. In fact, while America's first president was in office and the 300th anniversary of Columbus' discovery was approaching (1792), a movement arose to name America, "The United States of Columbia." The compromise was to name America's capital after America's two great heroes – "Washington, the District of Columbia" (now known as D.C.). The reason Columbus was chosen as a primary hero of America, on par with American Revolution hero, Washington, is not because he discovered America. It is because he was the man who started the idea that this westernmost land on earth was the fulfillment of end-times Bible prophecy.

As the Puritans planned their mission to the new world in the 1600s, they were at the leading edge of English thinking when

8

they conceived of American colonization as the planting of a "city on a hill," i.e. the Millennium. So, when Puritan leader, John Winthrop applied Christ's words, "a city on a hill" (Matthew 5:14) to the "howling wilderness" the Puritans were colonizing, it was not so much Winthrop's idea as it was the transporting of an English idea. The Puritan mission was not for the mere purpose of "religious freedom." Its goal was to plant authentic biblical Christianity in the wilderness and create the perfect "city on a hill" that Christ forecast in the Beatitudes. It was in part inspired by the Englishman Thomas More in his 1516 novel, *Utopia*. This book described a perfect society off the coast of America. This novel was based on the growing expectation of Christ's coming Millennium.

This idea of America as "a city on a hill" has taken root in America, becoming its metaphorical title lasting 350 years, up to the end of the 20th century. Two of America's most celebrated presidents, John F. Kennedy and Ronald Reagan, used the nickname repeatedly in famous speeches 20 years apart.

Daniel's Fifth Empire

The passage quoted most often by those who believe America is found in Bible prophecy is found in Daniel 2:34, 35:

> Thou sawest till that a stone was cut out without hands, which smote the image upon his feet that were of iron and clay, and brake them to pieces. Then there was the iron, the clay, the brass, the silver, and the gold, broken to pieces together, and became like the chaff of the summer threshingfloors; and the wind carried them away, that no place was found for them: and the stone that smote the image became a great mountain, and filled the whole earth.

According to this view, America is the fulfillment of the last of the five empires God prophesied through Daniel the prophet. America was the beginning of the "Stone Mountain" kingdom that would crush all the ancient empires from Babylon to Rome. America was to be the "vestibule" that would usher in the Millennium.

The American understanding of the USA as Daniel's "Stone Mountain" authorized early 19th century political ideas such as the Monroe Doctrine and "Manifest Destiny." Daniel says this empire will overspread the earth and both of the Democrat doctrines claimed the divine right to dominate, not just America, but the Americas. Without the widespread understanding of America as the outworking of the "Stone Mountain" prophecy, both of these political doctrines look like sheer arrogance and imperialism.

Berkeley's Poem Identifies America as the

Fulfillment of Bible Prophecy

The view of America as Daniel's fifth empire flowered in 1726 with a prophetic poem by one of Britain's greatest minds, Church of England Bishop George Berkeley (namesake of Berkeley, California). He predicted that Britain's American colonies would become the place where Daniel's "Stone Mountain," the last great empire of history, would arise. This had an electric effort on America's spiritual leaders, from Jonathan Edwards into the 20th century.

It was the last stanza of Berkeley's poem, "Verses on Planting the Arts and Learning in America" that awoke American leaders, like the ringing of a church bell at midnight:

"Westward the course of empire takes its way,

The First acts already passed;

The fifth shall close the drama of the day;

Time's noblest offspring is the last."

It is easy to decode this poem in the time context in which it was presented. To Berkeley, the idea of Daniel's fifth empire was unfolding in real time. Let's analyze each line:

(1) WESTWARD THE COURSE OF EMPIRE TAKES ITS WAY. Berkeley is combing the ancient idea of time and history following the western trajectory of the heavenly bodies with Daniel's Five-Empire prophecy. He poetically portrays these empires and constellations with the word, "course." The sun, moon and stars follow a daily western "course." America is the westernmost body of land on earth. If Japan is the 'land of the rising sun,' America is the 'land of the setting sun,' the place history will end.

(2) THE FIRST FOUR ACTS ALREADY PASSED. English speaking people would immediately understand Berkeley was referring to Daniel's first four empires (Babylon, Medo-Persia, Greece and Rome) with the phrase, "The first four acts already passed." Everybody knew those first four empires had already come and gone. Europe had been awaiting the last empire for more than two centuries when Berkeley wrote this poem.

(3) THE FIFTH SHALL CLOSE THE DRAMA WITH THE DAY. Using the term, "the fifth" pointed to Daniel's Fifth Empire, which would be the last,

according to God's prophecy to Daniel. The "Stone Mountain" would close God's drama; i.e., history, bringing the stumbling, bloody progression of this fallen world to a conclusion.

(4) TIME'S NOBLEST OFFSPRING IS THE LAST. This references Daniel's Fifth and last empire of history, the "Stone Mountain." Berkeley anoints America as Daniel's Fifth Empire.

Just as Berkeley predicted, America did become "time's noblest empire," History's Great Nation, i.e. Daniel's Fifth Empire. America became greater than all the ancient empires. It changed the world! Politically, America's model was instrumental in changing the world from what it was in 1726 when Berkeley penned his prophetic poem, a world exclusively ruled by monarchies. The world is now largely governed in the American style democratic electoral process – because of the model America gave the world. America's inventions in every area of human endeavor are largely responsible for the giant leap into modernity that has taken place.

The Belief that America is in Bible Prophecy in the 19th & 20th Century

For most of American history, from the Puritan colonization of New England well into the 20th century, the idea that America was God's country in the modern world, the fulfillment of Bible prophecy, was a major political doctrine. It was on full display particularly in the middle of the 19th century.

For example, in 1857, George Washington's birthday (February 21, 1735) was celebrated as follows: Southern minister, Reverend Fountain Pitts held an all-day seminar in the United

States Capital Building on "America's place and destiny in the Bible." It was a packed event of America's political ruling class in the place where they made America's laws. Rev. Pitts invoked the most definitive Bible prophecy of the United States of America. Pitt taught that America was the fulfillment of the last of the five empires God had given Daniel the prophet. America was the beginning of the "Stone Mountain" that would crush all the ancient empires from Babylon to Rome (Daniel 2:34, 35).

This view was prevalent through the balance of the 19th century and into the 20th century. In fact, this view was on display in the first presidential race of the 20th century. The American political-prophetic belief that America is Daniel's fifth empire was the theme of President William McKinley's 1900 re-election campaign. At the end of the 19th century, most Americans expected the 20th century to become the golden age of the Millennium, and perhaps the time when Christ would actually return. So, the theme of McKinley's campaign was that his presidency would be God's instrument to fulfill God's will for America. This view fit perfectly with the end-of-the-19th-century belief that the very best age of America was coming in the 20th century. It is upon this foundation of America's importance in end-times Bible prophecy that I will make my case that America is experiencing in our day, "A Nineveh Moment."

Editor's Note: The information in this chapter was gleaned from the articles "America is Forecast in Bible Prophecy, Parts I, II" by Paul Warren Dinger (*Last Days Beacon*, October, November 2018)

Chapter Two

HISTORICAL SETTING AND MODERN PARALLELS

One of the most amazing true stories in the Old Testament has to do with the Prophet Jonah's evangelistic ministry in the Assyrian city of Nineveh. During the reign of Jeroboam II (793-753 B.C.) Jonah was commissioned by God to ". . . go to Nineveh, that great city, and cry against it; for their wickedness is come up before me" (Jonah 1:2). After rebelling, fleeing and "reconsidering" God's commission while ensconced in the belly of a great fish, Jonah reluctantly concurred that he should obey the Lord. He entered Nineveh and warned, ". . . Yet forty days and Nineveh shall be overthrown" (Jonah 3:4). Then, an amazing thing happened: "So the people of Nineveh believed God and proclaimed a fast, and put on sackcloth, from the greatest of them even to the least of them. For word came unto the king of Nineveh, and he arose from his throne, and he laid his robe from him, and covered him with sackcloth, and sat in ashes" (Jonah 3:5-6). In response, the most astounding thing of all happened: "And God saw their works, that they turned from their evil way; and God repented of the evil, that he had said that he would do unto them; and he did it not" (Jonah 3:10).

This is a phenomenal turn of events! Nineveh was an extremely wicked city, full of immorality, idolatry and violence! It was the greatest of the Assyrian cities, founded by Nimrod himself (Genesis 10:8-12). It was untouched by Judaism. If any city was worthy of annihilation by God, it was Nineveh. Then, for some inexplicable reason, God sent Jonah with a message of warning. Perhaps because his skin was bleached, giving him the appearance of an angel as a result of his visit to the whale's belly, Jonah garnered immediate attention when he traversed the great city. Whatever the case, God used the reluctant prophet to effect repentance and the city was spared God's judgment for over 100 years. It was not destroyed until 612 B.C., long after the Assyrian Empire swallowed up Israel in 722 B.C.

Is it possible that this historical example is being repeated in America? Could America be receiving a similar reprieve from the Lord? Could Donald Trump's election be a "Nineveh moment," a period of time when the judgment of God is delayed in order to leave space for repentance? If any nation has given cause for the judgment of God in recent years, it is America. I want to survey the moral boundaries America has crossed over the past 50 years or so that has placed it in the danger zone for the judgment of God. These are quoted from Bill Salus' excellent book, *The NOW Prophecies*:[1]

- 1962 – Engel v. Vitale: the removal of prayer in public schools by the Supreme Court.

- 1963 – Abington School District v. Schempp: the removal of Bible reading in public schools by the Supreme Court.

- 1973 – Roe v. Wade: legalized abortions by the Supreme Court. Since then, America has performed over 60 million abortions. Presently about one million abortions are occurring per year in America.

---

[1] Bill Salus, *The NOW Prophecies* (USA: Prophecy Depot Publishing, 2016) 64-65.

- 1980 – Stone v. Graham: in this case the Supreme Court ruled that a Kentucky statute was unconstitutional. The statute in question required the posting of a copy of the Ten Commandments on the wall of each public classroom in the state. The Court ruled that because they were being placed in public classrooms, they were in violation of the First Amendment.

- 2003 – Lawrence v. Texas: This was the landmark decision by the United States Supreme Court that struck down the sodomy law in Texas, which by extension, invalidated sodomy laws in 13 other states.

- 2013 – United States v. Windsor: the case in which the Supreme Court struck down the Defense of Marriage Act (DOMA). DOMA stated that one man should be married to one woman. DOMA was biblically supported according to Genesis 2:24, "Therefore a man shall leave his father and mother and be joined to his wife, and they shall become one flesh."

- 2015 - Obergefell v. Hodges: This was the Supreme Court case that ruled in favor of same sex marriages, which is unbiblical according to Romans 1:27 and elsewhere.

For these reasons, America, like Nineveh, has become a very wicked place, deserving of the judgment of God. In the next chapter, we will deal with the messengers, the "Jonahs," that have brought warning to America over the past 60 years or so.

Chapter Three

THE "JONAHS"

In the last chapter, I dealt with God's mercy toward Nineveh and applied it to the present moment in America's national history. With the election of Donald Trump as the 45th president of the United States, God may be granting us a "Nineveh moment." By that I mean a temporary reprieve from the judgment of God that America so richly deserves. I have previously listed the moral and biblical boundaries that America has crossed over the last 50 plus years that has put us in danger of experiencing the judgment of God.

In this chapter I want to chronicle some of the "Jonahs" that have been warning America of impending judgment and have been calling America back to its founding principles. This list is by no means comprehensive. Instead, it surveys those individuals and organizations that, in my opinion, have had the greatest influence in restoring America to its founding principles.

Robert Welch, Jr. (1899-1985): Welch is the founder of **The John Birch Society** (JBS). In 1958, Mr. Welch developed an organizational infrastructure of JBS chapters nationwide. JBS is a conservative educational and advocacy group supporting anti-communism and limited government. Headquartered in Appleton, Wisconsin, JBS owns American Opinion Publishing, which publishes the monthly magazine, *The New American.* They also have Freedom Project Academy, a K-12 online school for young American patriots. In my view, the John Birch Society is the patriarchal organization of modern-day Constitutional restoration movements in America. It is noteworthy that Fred Trump, father of President Trump, was an early supporter of Robert Welch and the John Birch Society.

Barry Goldwater (1909-1998): Barry Goldwater was an American politician and businessman who was a five-term United States Senator from Arizona and the Republican Party's nominee for President of the United Sates in the 1964 election. Despite losing the election in a landslide, Goldwater is the politician most often credited for sparking the resurgence of the American conservative political movement in the 1960s. Goldwater rejected the legacy of the New Deal and helped build the conservative coalition against the New Deal coalition.

Phyllis Schlafly (1924-2016): Phyllis was a Constitutional lawyer and conservative activist. In 1972 she founded what is now known as **The Eagle Forum**. The Eagle Forum is a conservative interest group in the United States and is the parent organization that also includes the **Eagle Forum Education and Legal Defense Fund** and the **Eagle Forum PAC**. She founded Eagle Forum in 1972 and remained its chairman and CEO until her death in September of 2016. The Eagle Forum has been primarily focused on social issues such as pro-life and pro-family and reports a membership of 80,000. This organization successfully led the fight against the ratification of the Equal Rights Amendment in the 1970s. Phyllis Schlafly endorsed Donald Trump and published her last book shortly before her death, entitled, *The Conservative Case for Trump.*

Ronald Reagan (1911-2004): Ronald Reagan was an actor and politician who was the 40th President of the United States. Before his presidency, he was the governor of California from 1967 to 1975, after a career as a Hollywood actor and union leader. In 1964, Reagan's speech, "A Time for Choosing," in support of Barry Goldwater's presidential campaign, earned him national attention as a new conservative spokesman. He ran unsuccessfully for the Republican nomination for the U.S. presidency in 1968 and 1976; four years later, he easily won the nomination and went on to overwhelmingly defeat incumbent Jimmy Carter in 1980. Entering the presidency in 1981, Reagan implemented sweeping new political and economic initiatives. His tax rate reduction and government regulatory relief spurred economic growth. Over his two terms, his economic policies saw a reduction of inflation from 12.5% to 4.4% and produced an average annual growth of real GDP of 3.4%. His robust foreign policy also resulted in the end of the Cold War and the subsequent fall of the Soviet Union. Many believe that the "Reagan Revolution" was the culmination of the conservative movement that began under Goldwater.

Ron Paul (1935-present): is an author, physician and former politician. He served as the U.S. Representative for Texas' 22nd congressional district (1976-77; 1979-85; 1997-2013). On three occasions, he sought the presidency of the United State: as the Libertarian Party nominee in 1988 and as a candidate in the Republican primaries of 2008 and 2012. Dr. Paul is a critic of the federal government's fiscal policies, especially the existence of the Federal Reserve, as well as the military-industrial complex that has spawned interventionist foreign wars. Dr. Paul has also been a vocal critic of mass surveillance policies such as the Patriot Act and the NSA surveillance program. Known as "Dr. No" in Congress, Dr. Paul is the only member of Congress over the last 50 years to have a *perfect voting record* in terms of Constitutional compliance. He is known as the "intellectual godfather" of the Tea Party movement and many believe that the "Ron Paul Revolution" of 2008-2012 set the stage for Trump's revolutionary victory in 2016.

It is my view that these individuals and organizations, among others, laid the essential foundations of Americanism and Constitutional government that the Trump Revolution was built upon. In the next chapter, I will give my view as to the "MVPs" in the stunning Trump electoral victory of 2016.

Chapter Four

THE "MVPS" OF THE
TRUMP MIRACLE

It is my view that, with the election of Donald Trump, God may be granting America a "Nineveh moment." By that I mean that the United States may be receiving a temporary reprieve from the judgment of God that we so richly deserve. I have listed the moral and biblical boundaries that America has crossed over the last 50 plus years that has put us in danger of experiencing the judgment of God. I have also profiled some of the "Jonahs" that having been warning American of impending judgment and have been calling America back to its founding principles over the last 60 years. God uses INDIVIDUALS that create MOVEMENTS that CHANGE HISTORY! Some of these "Jonahs" included Robert Welch Jr., Barry Goldwater, Phyllis Schlafly, Ronald Reagan and Ron Paul. I believe that these patriotic individuals, among others, laid the groundwork for the Trump Revolution.

In this chapter, I want to list some the "MVPs" that helped overcome two of the most powerful political dynasties in modern American history. The Bush and Clinton crime families have dominated American politics since the 1980s. Both well-connected globalist families have wielded great power in terms of their fund raising and media prowess. It was assumed by the "duopoly" parties and the mainstream media (MSM) that Jeb Bush and Hillary Clinton would be the nominees of their rigged system, thus guaranteeing that, whoever won, the one-worlders would continue to be in charge. Donald Trump dumped both families into the ash heap of history, at the same time overcoming a monopolistic and monolithic "mainstream" media industry determined to preserve the ruling oligarchy in America.

Ben Carson, a very successful neurosurgeon and Republican candidate for President stated, "Quite frankly, having an uninformed populace works extremely well, particularly when you have a media that doesn't understand its responsibility and feels more like it's an arm of a political party. They can really take advantage of an uninformed populace." So true! This election, in my view, turned into a rout of the establishment because of an "information war" waged by the independent alternative media to inform the electorate.

Donald Trump: At the outset, let me state that the leader in communicating the revolutionary "America First" message was, without question, Donald Trump himself! Defying all odds and overcoming opposition from every corner of the establishment, Mr. Trump selflessly, tirelessly and forcefully communicated his pro-America, pro-life, pro-prosperity message to massive crowds throughout this country. His Herculean effort enabled him to speak directly to more Americans than any candidate in American history. Some say that Trump is a "con-man" and a "demagogue." Time will tell, but in Donald Trump we have a successful businessman that did not need the presidency and all the attacks he has endured to achieve it. Yet he soldiered on with the whole globalist establishment arrayed against him. His message: "Americanism, not globalism, that is our credo!" How refreshing! At the same time he was barnstorming the country with his "America First" message, he was aided by several "MVPs" that assisted him in waging this information war. I will deal with them in no particular order.

 **Alex Jones**, founder and director of Infowars.com. In 1993, as a result of the government massacre of almost 100 men, women and children at the Branch Davidian Compound in Waco, Texas a young man from Austin, Texas began a show over a single cable access TV station. Since then, Alex Jones has grown a media empire that includes a daily syndicated radio show that is heard on over 160 radio stations, as well as an internet audience that reaches tens of millions of listeners weekly, plus multiple millions of viewers of his video documentaries. Alex is an ardent patriot who leverages his passion and energy to fight the New World Order. Early on in the Republican primaries Alex became convinced that Donald Trump was just what America needed. He mobilized America's patriots, sold "Hillary for Prison" and "Bill is a Rapist" T-shirts and even interviewed Mr. Trump for his vast radio and internet audience.

 **James O'Keefe**, founder of Project Veritas Action. James is a citizen journalist famous for his undercover investigations. It was Project Veritas that exposed the criminal behavior of ACORN, Obama's community organizing group several years ago. In this election cycle, the Project Veritas Action crew investigated the crimes of the DNC and the Clinton campaign. In a series of timely undercover videos Project Veritas

exposed the following: The Clinton Campaign, in concert with the DNC and the White House, paid and organized violent protestors at Trump rallies as well as conspired to commit election fraud. This undercover investigation created a major scandal within the Obama/Clinton criminal enterprise, resulting in the resignations of major leaders in the operation.

 **Roger Stone** is a conservative political insider and Republican strategist going all the way back to the Nixon years. Mr. Stone has been a close friend and confidant to Donald Trump for over 40 years, as well as an associate of Paul Manafort, who helped lead the Trump campaign to victory in the Republican primaries. Mr. Stone has encouraged Trump to run for President since 1988 and had served as chairman of his Presidential Exploratory Committee in 2000. In the 2016 election, Mr. Stone led the "Stop the Steal" effort by recruiting and training citizen "Poll Protectors" to do exit polling in critical swing states.

 **Steve Pieczenik** is also a long-term political insider going all the way back to the Nixon Administration. He served as Deputy Secretary of State under four administrations, as well as Senior Policy Planner under the Reagan administration. He has additionally served in many intelligence-related roles on behalf of the U.S. Government. Mr. Pieczenik, though retired from government service, is in close contact with patriots serving within our intelligence agencies. It was his leadership that assisted in the counter-coup that recently prevented Hillary Clinton from stealing the election. He revealed the fact that the Hillary damaging

WikiLeaks data released in the weeks prior to the election did not come from the Russians. In point of fact, this information was released by patriots within the Intelligence Community who were justifiably alarmed at the prospect of a Clinton presidency.

Julian Assange, Director of WikiLeaks. Since WikiLeaks founding in 2006, they have released millions of documents pertaining to the criminality of political leaders. In this election cycle, the release of thousands of emails pertaining to the Clinton campaign contributed greatly to uncovering criminal activity on the part of Hillary Clinton and her campaign staff. This information helped inform the American people and contributed to her ruinous defeat. Because of his courage and sense of duty, he has now been arrested and is facing extradition to the United States. The Deep State wants to silence Assange because of his effectiveness in exposing their crimes.

Seth Rich, Democratic National Committee (DNC) staffer. This 27-year old leaked internal documents to Wikileaks from the DNC proving that they worked with Hillary Clinton to steal the Democrat nomination from Bernie Sanders. The DNC became aware of Mr. Rich's actions and the Clinton "crime machine" flew into action, putting multiple bullets into Mr. Rich's back and killing him in the early morning hours of July 10, 2016 in downtown D.C. As a result of this information about the theft of Sander's nomination going public, DNC Chair Debbie Wasserman Schultz resigned, and Bernie Sanders' supporters literally walked out of the DNC Convention. Mr. Rich gave his life so that American citizens would know the truth!

Each of these individuals demonstrated courage and tenacity in the face of evil and tyranny. Each has been threatened in some way by the globalist establishment, but they did not quit. They did not merely *observe* tyranny, they did what they could to *expose* and *defeat* it. These men are the unsung heroes of the Trump Revolution. As Edmund Burke stated so well, "All that is required for evil to triumph is for good men to do nothing." Because these good men did SOMETHING, evil was defeated in the 2016 presidential election and America has another chance to restore the Republic. These are a few of the "info warriors" in the Second American Revolution. It is their efforts and the efforts of many other foot soldiers of liberty that are giving this country "A Nineveh Moment."

Chapter Five

THE JUDGMENT AVERTED

We began by looking at the story of Jonah and his evangelistic mission to the wicked city of Nineveh. This city was so wicked that Jonah's message was straightforward: "Yet forty days, and Nineveh shall be overthrown" (Jonah 3:4). We are not told the manner in which God would overthrow this vast city, but certainly the populace was aware of God's judgment on Sodom and Gomorrah. However they perceived that this overthrow would take place, the warning was effective: "So the people of Nineveh believed God, and proclaimed a fast, and put on sackcloth, from the greatest of them unto to the least of them. For word came unto the king of Nineveh, and he arose from his throne, and he laid his robe from him, and covered him with sackcloth, and sat in ashes" (Jonah 3:5-6).

It is my view that, America, like Nineveh, came very close to being "overthrown." If Hillary Clinton had succeeded in stealing the election, I believe it would have resulted in the final overthrow of America as a Christian Constitutional Republic. I believe that judgment has been averted, or at least delayed, because of the election of Donald Trump. Let me give several possible outcomes if Hillary had seized power:

1. OPEN BORDERS: Hillary Clinton has long been an advocate of open borders. In fact, it was her desire to increase the number of Syrian refugees from the 10,000

that Obama had promised, to 65,000, an over 550% increase. In fact, during this election, the Clinton campaign hired illegals to register other illegals to vote. It is estimated that approximately three million illegal aliens voted in the presidential election. You can guess who they voted for. The Democrat strategy, over at least the past eight years, has been to flood the country with millions of illegal immigrants, in order to make the Democrat party the permanent majority party in America. The continued open borders would have had several effects, beyond their current impact. First, it would have bankrupted our country by overwhelming our social services. This Cloward-Piven[2] strategy would bankrupt our public hospitals, schools and welfare systems. Second, it would drive down wages and deprive hard pressed Americans of jobs. Third, it would have resulted in an increase in terrorism on the order of what we are seeing in Europe. Fourth, it would have resulted in the permanent destruction of the Christian culture upon which our country was founded.

2. SUPREME COURT: With the suspicious death of Supreme Court Chief Justice, Antonin Scalia in 2015, President Trump was able to fill this opening with the successful appointment of Neil Gorsuch. Then, following the retirement of Justice Kennedy, Trump was able to fill this opening with the successful, yet highly contentious appointment of Brett Kavanaugh. His third conservative addition to the Supreme Court was Amy Coney Barrett. The conservative majority was able to overturn Roe v

---

[2] This is a political strategy to overload the American public welfare system to the point that it creates a crisis and bankrupts the nation, leaving the country no choice but to adopt a socialist/communist agenda.

Wade, returning the abortion issue to the states where it belongs. The addition of these conservative justices will tilt the court philosophically for the next 20 or more years. All of these are conservative, "original construction" judges.

Hillary, on the other hand, would certainly have nominated the most liberal, pro-abortion, anti-second amendment judges she could find. A Hillary presidency would, most likely, have resulted in the utter destruction of the Bill of Rights, delivering America to a Communist Chinese form of government. Mao Tse-tung killed 80 million Chinese in his "Cultural Revolution." (By the way, have you noticed Hillary's penchant for wearing Maoist-type pantsuits?) Is she a Communist Chinese agent? The Chinese government provided 300 million dollars for her presidential campaign. Remember that her husband also sold nuclear secrets to China to help finance his 1996 re-election campaign.

3. FIRST AMENDMENT DESTRUCTION: During her campaign, Hillary declared war on what she called "The Alt-Right." By that she meant the conservative Alternative Media that is rendering the dinosaur Mainstream Media extinct. She has specifically singled out Alex Jones, Matt Drudge and Steve Bannon in her criticism. In fact, in a recovered WikiLeaks document, she suggested that Julian Assange be murdered in a drone strike. Hillary is also suspected to be behind the mysterious death of Seth Rich, who leaked DNC documents to WikiLeaks pertaining to the theft of the DNC nomination from Bernie Sanders. Like all good communists, Hillary opposes free speech and, as president, would have been ruthless in shutting it down and silencing her opponents. Even after her defeat, she

continues to wage war against free speech by urging Congressional action against "fake news" (i.e. news which does not originate with the MSM).

4. CONTINUED FOREIGN AGGRESSION: Hillary Clinton is an unashamed and unrepentant warmonger. When she and her co-president Bill Clinton were in office, they prosecuted a war in Kosovo, killing thousands of civilians. She also led the aggression in Libya, resulting in the brutal death of Muammar Gaddafi as well as four Americans at the embassy in Benghazi. Tens of thousands of civilians have been murdered by Islamic terrorists in Libya after Hillary's aggression. She, along with Obama, is also responsible for the civil war in Syria that has killed hundreds of thousands of civilians since 2011. By the way, the Syrian civil war has also decimated the Christian population in Syria. President Trump is reducing the number of American troops in the Middle East and vows to bring all our troops home from Syria and Afghanistan.

5. NUCLEAR WAR WITH RUSSIA: Her bellicose foreign policy has brought the United States to the brink of a nuclear war with Russia. She has pushed for a no-fly zone in Syria, despite the fact that Russia was invited in by Assad to protect his besieged country. Russia has declared a no-fly zone over Syria in order to protect against further Western aggression, as well as assist in eliminating the U.S. backed terrorists that have invaded and ravaged Syria in an attempt to overthrow their democratically elected president. In fact, prior to the 2016 election, Russia was on the highest level of nuclear alert and had conducted nuclear war drills involving 40 million Russians. Since Trump's

election, the level of nuclear alert has been reduced from DEFCON 3 to DEFCON 5. Trump and Putin have already spoken since the election and have pledged to normalize relations between the two countries. I believe that Trump's election has taken us back from the brink of nuclear war that would have potentially destroyed all human life on this planet (except, of course, the globalists in their underground bunkers).

With the election of Donald Trump, by the grace and mercy of God, judgment has been averted. What have been the beneficial effects of Trump's election for the United States? That will be the subject of our next chapter.

Chapter Six

THE TRUMP BUMP

Trump was inaugurated in January 2017, and during most of his presidency he was hamstrung by the 35-million-dollar witch hunt known as the Mueller investigation. This exhaustive investigation, which sought to pressure Trump associates into lying about the president, eventuated in exonerating Trump from charges of colluding with Russia in the 2016 election. He has also endured constant criticism by the mainstream press, as well as unending obstruction and investigation by the Democrats in Congress. Despite these mammoth obstacles, consider just a few of Trump's accomplishments in office:

The Trump Economic Record

- President Trump pushed Congress to enact the largest tax cuts for the American people since President Reagan. He cut the top tax rate on businesses from 35% to 21% to make America an attractive place to build a business again. He has also slashed tax rates for citizens, as well as doubling the standard deduction and doubling the exemption amount for dependents. The sweeping tax overhaul prompted more than 700 companies to issue cash bonuses, pay raises and other benefits to their employees. Nearly 4 million Americans have benefited from higher take-home pay as a result of these tax cuts.
- President Trump has signed more laws to slash unnecessary federal regulations and bureaucratic red tape than any president

in American history. This slashing of regulations is saving American businesses more than $18 billion a year in costs.

- President Trump is accomplishing what no modern American president has been able to do, that of making America energy-independent. For the first time, America is meeting all of its own energy needs and is an exporter of American energy. The United States has become the world's leading crude oil producer, surpassing Russia and Saudi Arabia. According to the latest official report, U.S. crude output hit an all-time high, exceeding 11.5 million barrels per day in October 2018. As a result of increased domestic oil production, oil prices have taken a nosedive since peaking in early October 2018.Trump has likened the lower oil prices to tax cuts, as they are an important windfall for consumers and the overall economy.

- He has approved the building of the Keystone XL and Dakota Access pipelines (with American steel).

- President Trump has saved the American people $3 TRILLION DOLLARS over the next 10 years by withdrawing from the Paris climate accord.

- The economy under President Trump is growing twice as fast as it was under Barack Obama, and we have seen GROSS DOMESTIC PRODUCT grow at a rate of 3 percent during 2018. During the second quarter of 2018 the economy grew at the blockbuster pace of 4.2 percent.

- The U.S. economy has created more than 4.8 million new jobs in the first two years under President Trump, and the unemployment rate fell to 3.7 percent for the first time in nearly 50 years. Unemployment in the manufacturing sector has dropped to a record low of just 2.6%. The manufacturing industry posted net job gains of 284,000 in 2018, its best year since 1997.

- The stock market has hit historic highs more times than you can count during the Trump years. The Dow Jones Industrial Average is up by 30 percent since Election Day 2016.
- More than $8 TRILLION DOLLARS in new wealth has been created under president Trump.
- Average hourly wages are up. As a result, the median household income of middle-class families reached a record high in 2017. A Census Bureau survey showed the median household income rose to $61,372, from $60,309 a year earlier, when adjusted for inflation.
- Consumer confidence, which drives economic growth, is at an 18-year high under president Trump.
- Trump has sought to reign in the power of the Federal Reserve Bank by challenging Chairman Powell on interest rates.
- Two million Americans off food stamps. The number of Americans receiving food stamp benefits dropped to a six-year low during Trump's first year in office, reflecting a healthy jobs market and an improving economy. On average 42.2 million Americans received food stamps in 2017, down 11 percent from 2013. The food stamps program cost American taxpayers $68 billion in 2017. That's 15% less than the historical high of $79.9 billion in 2013.
- Opportunity zones. Created by Trump's tax reform, the "opportunity zones" program incentivizes Americans and foreigners to invest in economically underserved communities throughout the United States. The program offers tax incentives to private investors who invest in these zones. In 2018, the Treasury Department certified more than 8,700 distressed communities as qualified opportunity zones.

Trade

- NAFTA Replacement: The Trump administration landed its biggest trade win in 2018 by overhauling NAFTA. The new USMCA pact is a substantial improvement over NAFTA, and promotes production and jobs in the United States. The new rules, for example, incentivize the use of high-wage American manufacturing labor in the automotive sector.

- Trade War with China. Trump launched a tariff campaign in 2018 as part of a strategy to end China's unfair trade practices. As a result of these tariffs China has made a firm commitment to delivering structural changes with respect to forced technology transfer, intellectual property protection, cyber intrusions, and cyber theft of trade secrets.

- Ending TPP. Within three days of taking office, Trump withdrew the United States from the Trans-Pacific Partnership (TPP). The pact, negotiated under Obama, promised to boost trade between the 12 countries involved. However, some experts claimed that it would have zero effect on the U.S. economy.

- Steel and Aluminum Tariffs. The Trump administration launched an investigation in 2017 that concluded that dependence on imported steel and aluminum impaired national security. As a result, Trump signed orders imposing a 25 percent tariff on imported steel and a 10 percent tariff on imported aluminum in March 2018. Following the announcement of tariffs, U.S. metal manufacturers have started to reinvest in domestic production, creating new jobs.

- A new phase with Europe. Trump has renegotiated trade deals with the EU that has resulted in the EU's pledge to buy more soybeans and liquified gas from the U.S.

Ending Obamacare

When Congress was unable to get the votes to completely end Obamacare, President Trump canceled much of Obamacare on his own. Specifically, President Trump . . .

- Ended the billions of dollars in illegal taxpayer subsidies for insurance companies.
- Made it easier for lower-and middle-income citizens to buy plans that are half the cost of the Obamacare plans.
- Announced that the IRS will no longer fine people who don't have health insurance.
- Ended the outrageous Obama requirement that you must purchase health insurance for coverage of abortions.

Foreign Policy Victories

- The U.S. had been required by law to move the embassy from Tel Aviv after Congress adopted the Jerusalem Embassy Relocation Act in 1995. Previous presidents used waivers to postpone the move, citing national security interests. Trump successfully moved the American embassy from Tel Aviv to Jerusalem on May 14, 2018, Israel's 70th birthday.
- At his urging, NATO countries radically increased their defense spending, decreasing by billions of dollars the unfair share of defense spending borne by the U.S.
- He has defused tensions with North Korea because of personal diplomacy with Chairman Kim. This has not only averted war but has resulted in the regime slowing its provocative missile and nuclear tests. North Korea has also returned hostages and American remains from the Korean War.

- Securing release of American prisoners overseas. Not only did Trump secure the release of Otto Warmbier from North Korea, but also the release of prisoners from Turkey and China.
- Starting withdrawal of troops from Syria. In December of 2018 Trump announced the withdrawal of 2,000 U.S. troops from Syria, as he declared victory against the ISIS terrorist group, which now controls only one percent of the territory it once held during the Syrian civil war.

Military

- Increased funding for the military. Near the end of 2017, Trump signed a massive defense bill for 2018 that authorized about $700 billion for the Defense Department. This was an increase of $108 billion, or 18 percent, above the proposed 2017 budget.
- Modernizing of military equipment. Increased military spending has allowed the military to acquire large amounts of new defense equipment. Among the budgeted expenses are F-35 Joint Strike fighters, ground combat vehicles, and Virginia class submarines.

Law and Order

- During his first term, Trump signed numerous pieces of legislation committed to the abolition of human trafficking, making it a focal point of his administration. As a result, in 2018, ICE and Homeland Security investigations made 1,588 human trafficking arrests and over 8,500 human trafficking cases were reported to the National Human Trafficking Hotline.

- Criminal Justice Reform. Trump signed into law a landmark criminal justice reform bill dubbed the "First Step Act," on December 21, 2018. The bill gives judges more discretion when sentencing drug and lower-level offenders, while also working to reduce the recidivism risk of prisoners by expanding programs such as job training. It aims to make the federal criminal justice system fairer, reduce overcrowding, and save taxpayer dollars.

Cutting Waste

- Reducing U.N. Spending. Trump cut American contributions to the U.N budget by $285 million in the 2018-2019 fiscal year. The U.N. also cut $600 million from its annual peacekeeping budget of nearly $8 billion, following pressure from Trump.
- Slashing use of government time on union work. Trump, in an executive order, significantly limited the amount of time that public employees can spend working for unions while still being paid by the government. The government expects the order to save taxpayers $100 million over the course of a year.
- Reducing the White House Payroll. Trump reduced the number of White House employees from 474 in 2016 under Obama to 377 in 2017. The number of staffers dedicated to First Lady Melania Trump in 2018 is three; Michelle Obama, had 12 staffers in 2016.

Space fails me to catalogue other victories Donald Trump has won on behalf of the American people. In our next chapter, I will suggest priorities for American Christians during this Nineveh moment.

Chapter 7

WHAT DO WE DO NOW?

We began by looking at the true story of Jonah, who, in the 8th century B.C., was sent by the Lord on an evangelistic mission to Nineveh. This city was so wicked that Jonah's message was straightforward: "Yet forty days, and Nineveh shall be overthrown" (Jonah 3:4). We are not told the manner in which the overthrow would take place, but the message was effective: "So the people of Nineveh believed God, and proclaimed a fast, and put on sackcloth, from the greatest of them unto the least of them" (Jonah 3:4). We do know that, in the case of Nineveh, judgment was averted for over 100 years.

The city of Nineveh later fell to the Babylonians in 612 B.C. At that time, the city became an utter desolation and its palaces and temples were torn down. Zephaniah predicted this destruction: "And he will stretch out his hand . . . and destroy Assyria; and will make Nineveh a desolation, and dry like a wilderness . . . This is the rejoicing city that dwelt carelessly, that said in her heart, I am, and there is none beside me: how is she become a desolation, a place for beasts to lie down in! every one that passeth by her shall hiss, and wag his hand" (2:13, 15). History reveals that Nineveh's repentance was short-lived and that judgment averted merely became judgment delayed.

This kind of destruction may certainly prove to be the case in America in the future. It appears that, with the election of

Donald Trump, the overthrow of this country that would have surely occurred under Hillary Clinton has been averted for the time being. For how long and to what measure judgment will be averted in America lies in the mysterious realm called "the future." However, based on biblical history, the actions of man do influence the decisions of God, as seen in the Jonah narrative. That being said, what actions do I believe will avert, or at least delay, the judgment of God on our beloved country? Let me suggest a few:

1. REPENTANCE: This was the immediate response of the Ninevites. Repentance averted the impending judgment of God. Notice the proclamation of the king of Nineveh: "And he caused it to be proclaimed and published through Nineveh by the decree of the king and his nobles, saying, Let neither man nor beast, herd nor flock, taste any thing: let them not feed, nor drink water: But let man and beast be covered with sackcloth, and cry mightily unto God: yea, let them turn every one from his evil way, and from the violence that is in their hands. Who can tell if God will turn and repent, and turn away from his fierce anger, that we perish not? And God saw their works, that they turned from their evil way; and God repented of the evil, that he had said that he would do unto them; and he did it not" (Jonah 3: 7-10).

Repentance is the first order of business for the Laodicean Church in America. Repentance is defined in the *Evangelical Dictionary of Theology* as: ". . .that inward change of mind, affections, convictions, and commitment rooted in the fear of God and sorrow for offenses committed against him, which, accompanied by faith in

44

Jesus Christ, results in an outward turning from sin to God and his service in all of life."[3] In my view, the Laodicean Church in America has been far too concerned about entertaining and pacifying their congregations for the sake of institutional advancement, and far too unconcerned about reclaiming America for Christ. I say this as one who served as a full-time pastor for over 25 years.

Christians, individually and collectively, need to turn from their evil and violent ways, as the king of Nineveh wisely instructed his people. I believe this turning from violence needs to be reflected in America's foreign policy as well. Since the 9-11 false flag event, America has been on a rampage of aggression unlike any country since the Axis Powers in World War II.[4]

National aggression invites the judgment of God as we have seen throughout biblical history and church history! Following Jonah's ministry, Nineveh later became the capital of the Assyrian Empire. Assyria's subsequent aggression against neighboring countries eventually resulted in the judgment of God upon Nineveh; indeed, the

---

[3] Walter A. Elwell, *Evangelical Dictionary of Theology* (Grand Rapids: Baker Book House, 1984) 936.

[4] *The Project for the New American Century*, established in 1997 as the neoconservative think tank whose stated goal was to usher in a "new American century." Having won the cold war and with no military threat to speak of, this group of ideologues created a blueprint for the future whose agenda was to capitalize upon our surplus of military forces and funds and to force American hegemony and corporate privatization throughout the world. According to their own document, *Rebuilding America's Defense: Strategies, Forces, and Resources For a New Century,* (September, 2000) their stated goals would never be realized ". . . absent some catastrophic catalyzing event – like a new Pearl Harbor" (p. 51). www.oldamericancentury.org\pnac.htm

entire Assyrian empire was destroyed. God has judged every aggressive, warlike empire in history, whether it be Egypt, Assyria, Babylon, Greece, Rome, Spain, England, France, Germany or Japan. Do we think that the Lord, who is no respecter of persons or nations, will spare America for its rapacious destruction of multiple nations in the Middle East since the false flag attack on 9-11 and the invention of "the war on terror?"[5] The American war machine has been simultaneously waging war in multiple countries since 9-11. The Neo-Conservatives who have run our government since 2001 need to be rooted out, and I am hopeful that, under Donald Trump's leadership, that this will take place.[6]

If repentance by the millions of Christians in America is accompanied by evangelism, we may be on the cusp of experiencing America's Third Great Awakening.[7] May that be the subject of our earnest prayers!

2. PRAY FOR PRESIDENT TRUMP: The globalists who hijacked our country over the last 100 plus years are in full panic. They thought that their control of the duopoly parties and the mainstream media was sufficient to keep Trump from winning the election. They were wrong!

---

[5] An excellent treatment of the real causes and culprits of the 9-11 attack is revealed in the book entitled, *The War on Terror* by Christopher Bollyn. (Christopher Bollyn, 2017).

[6] An excellent book detailing the destructive influence of "Neo-Conservatives" in American government is entitled, *The High Priests of War* by Michael Collins Piper. (Washington, D.C.: American Free Press, 2004).

[7] The First Great Awakening took place in New England from 1740 to 1742. The Second Great Awakening took place in New England and the Midwest from the 1790s to 1840.

Truth be told, he won in a landslide, as impartial polls showed Trump was ahead by about 70 percent to Hillary's 20 percent (about 10% voted for other candidates). He also received over 76 million votes in 2020 and the election was stolen. Now that he is heading toward his third election, they will probably attempt to do a couple things. First, they will try to *eliminate* him. That is always in their deck of cards when they have a president they cannot control. Remember Kennedy and Reagan? The ones who orchestrated these events are the same Illuminati families that are running the show behind the scenes today. They are experts at assassination. There have already been multiple attempts on Trump's life during the campaign and during his time in office. Why do you think Trump orders fast food? He is rightfully concerned about being poisoned, one of the globalist's favorite methods of eliminating "obstacles." Second, they will try to *infiltrate* him with fake conservatives.

3. PROSECUTE THE CLINTONS: Justice in America is in tatters as a result of the Clinton crimes, which are too numerous to reiterate. It is obvious to any observer that the leadership of the Department of Justice and Federal Bureau of Investigation is still infected with Deep State operatives. There is, indeed, two standards of justice in America. The protected ruling class (the 1%) can literally get by with murder while the "deplorables" (the 99%) have no protections against the government. It is a despicable fact that no federal official has been sent to prison since the Watergate years! This has got to change; otherwise, our country will inevitably descend into utter chaos and lawlessness.

For the sake of justice in America, Trump needs to order his Attorney General to appoint a Special Prosecutor and Grand Jury to investigate and prosecute the multiple felonies of the Clintons. During the first Trump campaign, millions of Americans have been crying out for the need to "lock her up." This is a cry for JUSTICE! Only by meting out justice to the Clintons and their criminal cabal, will President Trump send a clear message that corruption, even at the highest levels of government, will be punished.

With the collapse of the "Russiagate Scandal," it is also time to investigate the investigators, and prosecute officials, both high and low, that undertook the overthrow of the duly elected President of the United States.

4. EMBRACE PUBLIC SERVICE: Christians have, for too long, viewed politics as a "dirty business." Pastors have encouraged political passivity in the pews; promoting vocational Christian service as being limited to pastors and missionaries. Hogwash! Civil service is an exalted calling, and pastors should encourage and support congregants in this holy calling. Only by Spirit-filled believers running for and attaining public office will righteous government be secured in the long-term. We need to return to the founder's vision of "citizen-politicians," patriots who leave their normal pursuits for a time to engage in the holy calling of civil service. We need to see more pastors set the example by running for political office!

5. RECLAIM PUBLIC EDUCATION: President-elect Trump has stated that he wants to abolish Common Core

and return school choice to Americans. His novel and practical concept is that educational money should follow the student, whether into homeschooling, parochial schools, charter schools or public schools. This concept of true "school choice" should lead to a resurgence of the homeschool and Christian school movement. This will, in the long-term, help reverse the Marxist indoctrination that millions of public-school children have been subjected to in this country.

I believe that the election of Donald Trump, more than anything else, was a miracle of God! Yes, human effort was involved, but, when all was said and done, God answered the prayers of his people around the world! The following Appendix will detail this election night miracle.

The Lord, in His mercy, has granted America a "Nineveh Moment," a moment of mercy, for Americans to repent, return to faith in the Lord Jesus Christ, and time to restore the Republic to its Constitutional roots. This moment may never come again. Trump is not a perfect man, but he is our last best hope to restore America. He loves America, He is not out to get us, and he does not have to do this. He could be living his sunset years in the lap of luxury, enjoying his successes in the company of his family and friends. Instead, because of his love for America, he works 18-hour days, amidst much criticism and opposition, to make America great again. This is the President I have been praying for all my adult life! I plan to give, to pray, and to work to reelect Donald J. Trump. I trust you will join me in this historic campaign, as we seek to extend "a Nineveh moment" for America.

APPENDIX I: SIGNS OF DIVINE INTERVENTION IN TRUMP VICTORY

Reprinted by permission from World Net Daily

Bachmann prayed with millions at crucial moment tide turned
Published: 11/09/2016 at 8:45 PM

By Garth Kant

WASHINGTON – Election eve 2016 began without any real sign of a gathering storm. No hint a popular revolt was brewing. In fact, just the opposite.

The networks were reporting the mood in the inner circle of the Republican candidate was subdued, somber, tense, even foreboding – as if fearing the worst.

In direct contrast, the mood in the camp of the Democratic Party presidential candidate was described as confident, expectant and already almost celebratory.

Giddy.

When the first polls closed on the East Coast and the first results began to come in, those moods seemed to be swiftly confirmed by reality. The pre-election polls were not wrong. Democratic Party nominee Hillary Clinton immediately took the lead.

And she was winning in the battleground states.

She was leading in Florida. She was leading in North Carolina. She was leading in Pennsylvania. She was leading in Ohio. Clinton was threatening to pull away and end the suspense early.

At 7 p.m., there was no sign of a popular uprising led by Republican presidential candidate Donald Trump. There was no sign at 8 p.m. There was still no sign as time inexorably marched on.

Something would have to break.

And then it did.

Like a scene out of the film "It's a Wonderful Life," people had begun to pray.

But not just in one small town. Across America. And around the world.

Simple acts of faith heralded the first faint wisps of a breeze that would soon become a storm that would shake the world.

It began in Jerusalem.

Christians from many nations gathered in the heart of Israel to pray and fast for the fate of the United States. Americans knelt on stage as the faithful prayed. Organizers instructed them to pray like never before for a just God to deliver his most Christian nation. They called it the Jerusalem Global Gathering.

Christians also gathered to pray for the nation outside the U.S. Capitol. As WND reported, pastor Dan Cummins of the small rural East Texas town of Bullard led prayers for a return to biblical principles.

JoAnn and Dan Cummins lead prayers on election
night in front of the U.S. Capitol

And it was in Texas that the prayers for deliverance were sent
around the world, using modern technology.

A large prayer group had gathered in Dallas, hosted by Ken
Copeland ministries. It was broadcast by the Daystar channel.
Presenters David Barton and former Rep. Michele Bachmann, R-
Minn., invited viewers to join in prayer.

Daystar has a global reach of 400 million potential viewers.

As they prayed, something began to stir.

"At the precise moment we began broadcasting on Daystar,"
Bachmann told WND, "as the polls were still open, and a national
audience of believers joined together and prayed in concert, we
literally saw the race break in favor of Trump."

"At that very minute."

She presented proof.

"The New York Times documented the shift in voting from that minute."

Chance of Winning Presidency

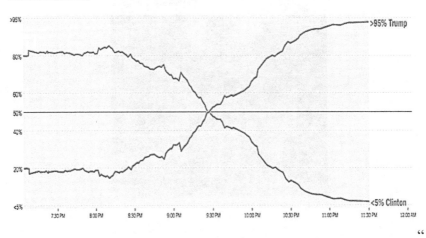

The Times put out a timeline tracking the election results as they broke for Trump last night," Bachmann continued. "We went wild in the Dallas studio last night when David Barton, Ken and Terri Copeland, and various pastors saw that the victory for Trump began exactly at the precise moment believers corporately, over national television, sought the Lord for His favor upon our nation."

"We knew it was at the exact same time that believers joined in corporate prayer on behalf of voting for a godly platform. Believers brought the Lord into this election, and that made all the difference," added the devout believer.

"That is the story of last night's victory. I have no doubt. The strong right arm of a holy God heard the prayers of His people and graciously answered our prayers," Bachmann reflected.

"It truly explains the Trump victory. I have no doubt. No man can take the credit. Only the strong right arm of a merciful God."

President-elect Donald Trump giving his victory speech

But that was in harmony with the "believers interceding on behalf of the American election last night in Jerusalem, praying in concert with those of us praying in America."

And there is no doubt someone was listening.

In addition to the hundreds-of-millions of viewers within Daystar's reach, the event drew about a million views online.

Bachmann said there had been a genuine repentance and coordinated beseeching of God. She told WND, "We saw the effective fervent prayers of righteous believers availing much."

"And, prayers so specific," she explained, "we prayed for elections by county and cities and districts. We literally watched results follow the faithful effectual prayers of righteous people who had humbled themselves and cried out to God for his mercy. This wasn't credit for us; this was clearly the Lord's gracious doing."

Bachmann proclaimed, "It is the story of the night and the biggest story of the year. I have no doubt."

"We were told more believers came out to vote in this election than ever before," she reflected, and the numbers confirmed that.

Trump benefited from the largest evangelical turnout in history.

Exit polls showed that an overwhelming 80 percent of white evangelical voters (who made up 25 percent of all 2016 voters) supported Trump.

Evangelicals of color preferred Clinton, but she did not get the same support from Hispanics and African-Americans as did President Obama.

Polls also showed that Trump recaptured the Catholic vote for the GOP by a margin of 52 percent to 45 percent, after most of them voted for Obama in the two previous presidential elections.

Bachmann said all of this "shows the necessity of believers voting for biblical principles in the voting booth."

Despite the victory, she concluded the work has just begun for the faithful, as well as the president-elect.

"This is not the time for believers to celebrate and turn away from doing our part affecting our society with the salt and light found in the Bible."

"Now is the time," she continued, "for pastors to preach biblically from America's pulpits on the various issues we confront in America."

"This is a beginning for people of faith. It is an opportunity to share the gospel and educate people on the fundamental primacy of the foundation of western civilization: The Bible."

APPENDIX II: TEXT OF DONALD TRUMP'S JULY 4, 2019 ADDRESS

Editor's Note: *On July 4, 2019, President Trump revived a tradition last seen by President Truman during the Korean war. This tradition is a presidential address on Independence Day.*

Hello, America. Hello. The First Lady and I wish each and every one of you a Happy Independence Day on this truly historic Fourth of July! Today, we come together as one nation with this very special Salute to America. We celebrate our history, our people, and the heroes who proudly defend our flag -- the brave men and women of the United States Military. . .

Together, we are part of one of the greatest stories ever told: the story of America. It is the epic tale of a great nation whose people have risked everything for what they know is right and what they know is true. It is the chronicle of brave citizens who never give up on the dream of a better and brighter future.

And it is the saga of thirteen separate colonies that united to form the most just and virtuous republic ever conceived. On this day, 243 years ago, our Founding Fathers pledged their lives, their fortunes, and their sacred honor to declare independence and defend our God-given rights. Thomas Jefferson wrote the words that forever changed the course of humanity: "We hold these truths to be self-evident: that all men are created equal, that they are endowed by their Creator with certain unalienable Rights, that among these are Life, Liberty, and the pursuit of Happiness." With a single sheet of parchment and 56 signatures, America began the greatest political journey in human history.

But on that day, the patriots who would determine the ultimate success of the struggle were a hundred miles away in New York.

There, the Continental Army prepared to make its stand, commanded by the beloved General George Washington. As the delegates debated the Declaration in Philadelphia, Washington's army watched from Manhattan as a massive British invading fleet loomed dangerously across New York harbor. The British had come to crush the revolution in its infancy. Washington's message to his troops laid bare the stakes. He wrote: "The fate of unborn millions will now depend, under God, on the courage and conduct of this army . . . We have, therefore, to resolve to conquer or die." Days later, General Washington ordered the Declaration read aloud to the troops.

The assembled soldiers just joined an excited crowd running down Broadway. They toppled a statue of King George and melted it into bullets for battle. The faraway King would soon learn a timeless lesson about the people of this majestic land: Americans love our freedom and no one will ever take it away from us. That same American spirit that emboldened our founders has kept us strong throughout our history.

To this day, that spirit runs through the veins of every American patriot. It lives on in each and every one of you here today. It is the spirit of daring and defiance, excellence and adventure, courage and confidence, loyalty and love that built this country into the most exceptional nation in the history of the world, and our nation is stronger today than it ever was before.

It is its strongest now. That same righteous American spirit forged our glorious Constitution. That rugged American character led the legendary explorers, Lewis and Clark, on their perilous expedition across an untamed continent. It drove others to journey West and stake out their claim on the wild frontier.

Devotion to our founding ideals led American patriots to abolish the evil of slavery, secure civil rights, and expand the blessings of liberty to all Americans. This is the noble purpose that inspired Abraham Lincoln to rededicate our nation to a new birth of freedom, and to resolve that we will always have a government of, by, and for the people.

Our quest for greatness unleashed a culture of discovery that led Thomas Edison to imagine his lightbulb, Alexander Graham Bell to create the telephone, the Wright Brothers to look to the sky and see the next great frontier. For Americans, nothing is impossible. Exactly 50 years ago this month, the world watched in awe as Apollo 11 astronauts launched into space with a wake of fire and nerves of steel, and planted our great American flag on the face of the moon . . .

Our nation's creativity and genius lit up the lights of Broadway and the soundstages of Hollywood. It filled the concert halls and airwaves around the world with the sound of jazz, opera, country, rock and roll, and rhythm and blues. It gave birth to the musical, the motion picture, the Western, the World Series, the Super Bowl, the skyscraper, the suspension bridge, the assembly line, and the mighty American automobile.

It led our citizens to push the bounds of medicine and science to save the lives of millions. Here with us this evening is Dr. Emmanuel Freireich. When Emmanuel began his work, 99 percent of children with leukemia died. Thanks largely to Dr. Freireich's breakthrough treatments, currently 90 percent of those with the most common childhood leukemias survive.

Doctor, you are a great American hero. Thank you. Americans always take care of each other. That love and unity held together the first pilgrims, it forged communities on the Great Plains, it inspired Clara Barton to found the Red Cross, and it keeps our nation thriving today. Here tonight from the Florida panhandle is Tina Belcher.

Her selfless generosity over three decades has made her known to all as "Mrs. Angel." Every time a hurricane strikes, Mrs. Angel turns her tiny kitchen into a disaster relief center. On a single day after Hurricane Michael, she gave 476 people a warm meal. Mrs. Angel, your boundless heart inspires us all. Thank you.

From our earliest days, Americans of faith have uplifted our nation. This evening, we are joined by Sister Deirdre Byrne. Sister Byrne is a retired Army surgeon who served for nearly 30 years. On September 11th, 2001, the sister raced to Ground Zero. Through smoke and debris, she administered first aid and comfort to all.

Today, Sister Byrne runs a medical clinic serving the poor in our nation's capital. Sister, thank you for your lifetime of service. Thank you. Our nation has always honored the heroes who serve our communities: the firefighters, first responders, police, sheriffs, ICE, Border Patrol, and all of the brave men and women of law enforcement.

On this July 4th, we pay special tribute to the military service members who laid down their lives for our nation. We are deeply moved to be in the presence this evening of Gold Star families whose loved ones made the supreme sacrifice. Thank you. Thank you. Thank you very much. Throughout our history, our country has been made ever greater by citizens who risked it all for equality and justice.

100 years ago this summer, the women's suffrage movement led Congress to pass the constitutional amendment giving women the right to vote. In 1960, a thirst for justice led African American students to sit down at the Woolworth lunch counter in Greensboro, North Carolina. It was one of the very first civil rights sit-ins and it started a movement all across our nation.

Clarence Henderson was 18-years-old when he took his place in history. Almost six decades later, he is here tonight in a seat of honor. Clarence, thank you for making this country a much better place for all Americans. In 1963, Reverend Martin Luther King, Jr., stood here on these very steps and called on our nation to live out the "true meaning of its creed," and "let freedom ring" for every citizen all across our land.

America's fearless resolve has inspired heroes who defined our national character -- from George Washington, John Adams, and Betsy Ross, to the great Frederick Douglas, Harriet Tubman, Amelia Earhart, Douglas MacArthur, Dwight Eisenhower, Jackie Robinson, and, of course, John Glenn.

It has willed our warriors up mountains and across minefields. It has liberated continents, split the atom, and brought tyrants and empires to their knees. Here with us this evening is Earl Morse. After retiring from the Air Force, Earl worked at a VA hospital in Ohio. Earl found that many World War Two veterans could not afford to visit their memorial on the National Mall.

Today, just as it did 243 years ago, the future of American freedom rests on the shoulders of men and women willing to defend it. We are proudly joined tonight by heroes from each branch of the U.S. Armed Forces, including three recipients of the Congressional Medal of Honor. Thank you. Thank you. They, and thousands before us, served with immense distinction, and they loved every minute of that service.

To young Americans across our country, now is your chance to join our military and make a truly great statement in life. And you should do it. We will now begin our celebration of the United States Armed Forces, honoring each branch's unique culture, rich history, service song, and distinct legacy. . . In August of 1790, by request of George Washington and Alexander Hamilton, Congress established a fleet of ten swift vessels to defend our shores.

These Revenue Cutters would fight pirates, stop smugglers, and safeguard our borders. They are the ancestors of our faithful Coast Guard. When our ships were seized and sailors kidnapped by foreign powers in 1812, it was a Revenue Cutter -- the swift schooner Thomas Jefferson -- that swept in to capture the first British vessel of the war.

In 1897, when 265 whalers were trapped in ice -- and the ice fields of Alaska were closing up -- courageous officers trekked fifteen hundred miles through the frozen frontier to rescue those starving men from a certain death. In 1942, the Coast Guard manned landing craft for invasions in the Pacific. When the enemy attacked U.S. Marines from the shores of Guadalcanal, Coast Guard Signalman First Class Douglas Munro used his own boat to shield his comrades from pounding gunfire.

Munro gave his life; hundreds of Marines were saved. As he lay dying on the deck, his final question embodied devotion that sails with every Coast Guardsman: "Did they get off?" On D-Day, the Coast Guard's famous Matchbox Fleet served valiantly through every hour of the greatest amphibious invasion in the history of our country.

One coxswain said "the water boiled with bullets like a mud puddle in a hailstorm," but still the Coast Guard braved death to put our boys on Utah and Omaha beaches. Every Coast Guardsman is trusted to put service before all. Coasties plunge from helicopters, and barrel through pouring rain and crashing waves to save American lives.

They secure our borders from drug runners and terrorists. In rough seas, at high speeds, their sharpshooters take out smugglers' engines with a single shot. They never miss. When the red racing stripes of a Coast Guard vessel break the horizon, when their chopper blades pierce the sky, those in distress know that the help is on their way, and our enemies know their time has come.

These guardians of our waters stand, "Semper Paratus." They are always ready. They are the United States Coast Guard. Representing the Coast Guard today, you will soon see an HH-60 Jayhawk helicopter based at Coast Guard Air Station Clearwater, along with an HH-65 Dolphin from Air Station Atlantic City, and an HC-144 Ocean Sentry from Air Station Miami.

Thank you. Thank you to the Coast Guard. On a cold December morning in 1903, a miracle occurred over the dunes of Kitty Hawk, North Carolina, when two bicycle makers from Ohio defied gravity with a 12-horsepower engine, wings made of cotton, and just a few dollars in their pockets.

Just six years later, America was training its first pilots to take these magnificent machines up and over the field of battle. In World War One, our flyboys rushed the skies of Europe, and aces like Eddie Rickenbacker filled hearts and headlines with tales of daring duels in the clouds. General Billy Mitchell saw the promise of this technology, and risked court martial in his quest for an independent air force.

He was proven right when empires across the oceans tried to carve up the world for themselves, and America stood in the way. We wouldn't let it happen. After Pearl Harbor, Lieutenant Colonel James Doolittle and his raiders flew B-25 bombers off a carrier deck in the deep Pacific in a daring feat of American resolve. And, as President Roosevelt said, the Nazis built a fortress around Europe, "but forgot to put a roof on it." So, we crushed them all from the air. One hundred and seventy-seven Liberator Bombers flew dangerously low, through broad daylight without fighter protection, to cripple the Nazi war machine at Ploiesti. More than 300 airmen gave their lives to destroy the enemy oil refineries.

And five pilots were awarded the Congressional Medal of Honor for their actions in that single raid. It was airman Chuck Yeager who first broke the sound barrier. It was airmen like Gus Grissom and Buzz Aldrin, who traded their Sabre jets for rockets to the stars. And it is our incredible airmen today who wield the most powerful weapons systems on the planet Earth.

For over 65 years, no enemy air force has managed to kill a single American soldier because the skies belong to the United States of America. No enemy has attacked our people without being met by a roar of thunder, and the awesome might of those who bid farewell to Earth, and soar into the wild blue yonder.

They are the United States Air Force. Representing the Air Force, you will soon see beautiful, brand new F-22 Raptors from Langley Air Force Base in Virginia -- and one magnificent B-2 Stealth Bomber from Whiteman Air Force Base in Missouri.

What a great country. In October of 1775, the Continental Congress ordered the construction of two swift-sailing vessels, each carrying 10 cannons and 80 men, to sail eastward. Our young fleet tested their sea legs against the most powerful navy the world had ever seen. John Paul Jones, America's first great naval hero, said: "I wish to have no connection with any ship that does not sail fast; for I intend to go in harm's way." He got his wish many times when his ship was shot into pieces off the coast of England by a British vessel and her four dozen guns.

When demanded to surrender, Jones very famously declared "I have not yet begun to fight!" When our Navy begins fighting, they finish the job. The War of 1812: Captain James Lawrence fell with his brothers on USS Chesapeake. His dying command gained immortality, "Don't give up the ship." In the Battle of Mobile Bay, Admiral David Farragut lashed himself to the rigging of his flagship to see beyond the cannon smoke, crying, "Damn the torpedoes, full speed ahead." In World War Two, it was aviators launched from the carrier Enterprise, Hornet, and Yorktown who filled the skies of Midway and turned the tide of the Pacific War.

Nobody could beat us. Nobody could come close. On D-Day, Seabee engineers came ashore to destroy blockades and barriers, making way for the invasion. Many lost their lives, but they took the German defenses with them, and our men rushed upon the beaches like a mighty storm. From the Naval demolition units of

World War Two arose a force that became famous in the Mekong Delta.

They don't want to see our force again. The very best of the very best: The Navy SEALs. It was the SEALs who delivered vengeance on the terrorists who planned the September 11th attack on our homeland. It was the SEALs who stand ready to bring righteous retribution -- in mountain, jungle, desert -- to those who do us harm.

America's sailors are not born. They are forged by the sea. Their traditions are rich with the salt and blood of three centuries. When Old Glory crests the waves of foreign shores, every friend and every foe knows that justice sails those waters. It sails with the United States Navy. Representing our great Navy today will be two F-18 Super Hornets from Naval Air Station Oceana in Virginia, along with two F-35 Lightning's from Naval Air Station Lemoore in California . . .

In November of 1775, the Continental Congress created two battalions of a new kind of warrior -- one who kept and would protect our ships and sailors, and be at home both ashore and in the mast, with musket in hand. Their versatility was proven in the War of Independence, when 234 Continental Marines conducted their first amphibious raid, capturing the British supply of gunpowder and cannons at Fort Nassau.

Ever since, Marines have fought in every American war. Their legend has grown and grown and grown with each passing year. It was the Marines who won America's first overseas battle, vanquishing Barbary pirates on the shores of Tripoli. Their high, stiff collar, which shielded them from the pirates' sword, earned them the immortal name: Leatherneck.

It was the Marines who, after two long days of battle, marched through the Halls of Montezuma. It was the Marines who took heavy casualties to kick the Kaiser's troops out of Belleau Wood in

World War One, earning the title "Devil Dogs." And it was the Marines who raised the flag on the black sands of Iwo Jima.

From the Chosin Reservoir to Khe Sanh, from Helmand to Baghdad, Marines have struck fear into the hearts of our enemies and put solace into the hearts of our friends. Marines always lead the way. After the 1983 Marine barracks bombing in Beirut, which claimed the lives of 241 great U.S. servicemen, Marine Sergeant Jeffrey Nashton lay in bandages -- so badly wounded, barely alive.

When the Commandant of the Marine Corps came to visit his hospital, Sergeant Nashton had to feel the General's collar; he wanted to feel his four stars. He could not see and he could not speak. He signaled for pen and paper, and with shaking hand he wrote two words: "Semper Fi." That motto, Semper Fidelis -- "Always Faithful" -- burns in the soul of every Marine, a sacred promise the Corps has kept since the birth of our country.

They are the elite masters of air and land and sea, on battlefields across the globe. They are the United States Marines. Representing the Marine Corps today will be a brand new VH-92, soon to serve as Marine One -- along with two V-22 Ospreys from the famed HMX-1 helicopter squadron at Quantico, the "Nighthawks."

In June of 1775, the Continental Congress created a unified army out of the revolutionary forces encamped around Boston and New York, and named after the great George Washington, Commander-in-Chief.

The Continental Army suffered the bitter winter of Valley Forge, found glory across the waters of the Delaware, and seized victory from Cornwallis at Yorktown . . .

And at Fort McHenry, under the rockets' red glare, it had nothing but victory. And when dawn came, their Star-Spangled Banner waved defiant. At Shiloh, Antietam, and Gettysburg, our soldiers gave the last full measure of devotion for the true unity of our nation and the freedom of all Americans. In the trenches of World War One, an Army Sergeant named Alvin York faced an inferno of enemy fire and refused to retreat.

He said, "I won't leave. I won't stop." He shot his rifle 18 times, killing 18 of the enemy. When they fixed bayonets and charged, he killed seven more. The entire German machine gun battalion surrendered because of one man, Alvin York. A generation later, the Army returned to Europe, and embarked upon a great crusade

With knives and rifles in hand, the Rangers scaled the cliffs of Normandy. The 101st Airborne leapt into the danger from above, illuminated only by enemy flares, explosions, and burning aircraft. They threw back the Nazi empire with lightning of their own, from the turrets of Sherman tanks and the barrels of the M1 rifle.

In the darkness of the Battle of the Bulge, with Nazis on every side, one soldier is reported to have said: "They've got us surrounded again, the poor bastards." Outnumbered, American warriors fought through the bunkers of Pork Chop Hill and held the line of civilization in Korea. In the elephant grass of Vietnam, the First Cavalry made its stand amid a forest consumed in flame, with enemies at every single turn.

The Army brought America's righteous fury down to Al Qaeda in Afghanistan and cleared the bloodthirsty killers from their caves. They liberated Fallujah and Mosul, and helped liberate and obliterate the ISIS caliphate, just recently, in Syria. One hundred percent gone.

Through the centuries, our soldiers have always pointed towards home, proclaiming, "This We'll Defend." They live by the creed of Douglas MacArthur: "In war, there is no substitute for victory." They are the greatest soldiers on Earth.

Nearly 250 years ago, a volunteer army of farmers and shopkeepers, blacksmiths, merchants, and militiamen risked life and limb to secure American liberty and self-government. This evening, we have witnessed the noble might of the warriors who continue that legacy.

They guard our birthright with vigilance and fierce devotion to the flag and to our great country. Now we must go forward as a nation with that same unity of purpose. As long as we stay true to our cause, as long as we remember our great history, as long as we never ever stop fighting for a better future, then there will be nothing that America cannot do.

We will always be the people who defeated a tyrant, crossed a continent, harnessed science, took to the skies, and soared into the heavens because we will never forget that we are Americans and the future belongs to us. The future belongs to the brave, the strong, the proud, and the free. We are one people, chasing one dream, and one magnificent destiny.

We all share the same heroes, the same home, the same heart, and we are all made by the same Almighty God. And from the banks of the Chesapeake to the cliffs of California, from the humming shores of the Great Lakes to the sand dunes of the Carolinas, from the fields of the Heartland to the everglades of Florida, the spirit of American independence will never fade, never fail, but will reign forever and ever and ever.

RECOMMENDED READING

The following books will expand your understanding of the subject of The Nineveh Moment:

Bongino, Dan. & McAllister, D.C. *Spygate: The Attempted Sabotage of Donald J. Trump.* NY: Post Hill Press, 2018.

Former Secret Service agent Dan Bongino draws on his expert knowledge to expose deep state actors who employed manipulations, setups, and abuse of power in an attempt to sabotage the Trump campaign and presidency.

Corsi, Jerome. *Killing the Deep State.* West Palm Beach, FL: Humanix Books, 2018.

Investigative journalist and #1 *New York Times* bestselling author, Jerome Corsi, blows the lid off the secret conspiracy to destroy the Trump presidency. Corsi also provides a roadmap ensuring that the will of the people – through President Trump – succeeds.

Howard-Browne, Rodney. *The Killing of Uncle Sam.* Tampa, FL: River Publishing, 2018.

This book captures details of the last 200 years of American history. It dissects the "legalized" system of the private central banks that has gone unchecked, and delivers gut-wrenching truths about the real domestic and foreign enemies of the United States.

Maginnis, Robert. *The Deeper State.* Crane, MO: Defender, 2018.

Lieutenant Colonel Maginnis uses his insider government knowledge to detail the war on Trump by corrupt elites, secret societies, and the builders of an imminent final empire.

Stone, Roger. *The Making of the President, 2016.* NY: Skyhorse Publishing, 2017.

Roger Stone, bestselling author, longtime political advisor and friend to Donald Trump, as well as the consummate Republican strategist, offers the definitive examination of how Trump's campaign delivered a stunning victory that almost no one saw coming (except Roger Stone, of course).

Taylor, Mark & Colbert, Mary. *The Trump Prophecies.* Crane, MO: Defender, 2017.

This is the astonishing true story of Mark Taylor, who received a prophecy in 2011 that Donald Trump would be elected president. This book reveals prophecies concerning Trump's election and what is coming during the Trump presidency.

Trump, Donald. *The Art of the Deal.* NY: Ballantine Books, 1987.

This #1 national bestseller is a commonsense guide to personal finance. In this book, Trump reveals the "elements of the deal" that made him a billionaire and won him the White House.

Williams, J.B. & Harrington, Timothy. *Trumped: The New American Revolution.* Cheyenne, WY: Charters of Freedom Publishers, 2016.

Trumped is about a national movement to "make America great again," a second American Revolution to restore the Constitutional republic via a rebirth of the Republican Party, represented by the political establishment outsider Donald Trump.

Made in the USA
Monee, IL
11 April 2024

56348472R00042